Searching for Me

Emily Zell

BookLeaf Publishing

Presentation by *BookLeaf Publishing*

Web: www.bookleafpub.com

E-mail: info@bookleafpub.com

ISBN: 9789357211918

First edition 2023

DEDICATION

For my kids, Sophie and Patrick, for keeping me grounded- you guys are my world.

And to my Great Grandfather "Ted" for reminding me what bravery and courage is.

ACKNOWLEDGEMENT

Thank you to my parents, sisters and all of my family and friends who have supported me through thick and thin. You kept me going on my darkest days.
Thank you to my medical team, including you Jen, who keep me positive and on track.

Love (Optimism)

How will we learn to love,
if loving isn't taught?
Is it something we were born with,
or something that you caught?

How will we know what love is,
when it comes about?
Will it be floating feelings,
or will it just be doubt?

When does love come to us,
at morning or at night?
How will we know,
is it just through sight?

Whenever love comes around,
even if its pulled apart,
I'll greet it with my open arms
and lead it to my heart.

1999 (16 years old)

Sick (the crash)

You're so sick
your mind,
your heart,
you make me want to spew!

You never changed
how could you?
You'd never change
why would you?

Add me to your tally
and count 1,2,3
Add me to your followers
But why did you choose me?

2000 (17 years old)

Hurt You (hiding)

Just ignore what they say
Just ignore what they do
Don't beat yourself up
Don't listen- it's nothing new

Don't take it to heart
they don't mean to hurt you
Just let them say the things
What else could you do?

Don't worry 'bout the past,
or the future too.
Don't let everyone see
what they've done to you.

2001

For You (trying again)

What did I say?
What did I do?
Was it me,
or was it you?

What did happen
to make us this way?
Look at how
we are today!

Did I do something wrong?
Did I make you sad?
Did I hurt you,
or make you mad?

Did you not know?
Did you not care?
Did you lie,
Cause I was there?

I loved you then
from the start
You should know
you broke my heart

I hope that you are happy now
I hope that you find love
and in my broken heart I know,
It's you I'll always love.

2001

To Dream (memories)

I feel your arms wrap around me
your kiss behind my ear, and down my neck
you kiss my shoulder, before you pull the
blanket up to my chin

We can hear the wind outside and the birds up in
the trees,
the crackling of the fire and voices whispering in
the night

In this moment
I am warm,
I am safe
I am loved
I am free.

I hear you whispering to me and I snuggle in
closer as a tear slips down my cheek

I remind myself that
I am warm,
I am safe
I am loved
I am free.

... but I know that today will be our last day and
we won't get a tomorrow.
I know this, because I lived it

And sometimes I cry, for missing my chance,
but it won't bring you back
and we couldn't have made it work
Coz I know what I wanted,
and I knew you wanted something different.
I couldn't hold you back.

So sometimes when I'm in bed alone
I feel your arms wrap around me, your kiss
behind my ear
and I snuggle in closer, hearing your breath
whisper to me
"No matter where we end up, you'll always be
mine"
while a tear slips from my eye as I slip in to
sleep, to dream.

2019

The Visit (the hope)

7am
I wake up excited,
12 hours or so until I see you.
I wait for a message to say you're on your way

9am
A part of me really wants to know the answer,
but a part of me is scared.
Scared that you'll break your promise,
and I'll break instead.

10am
I just sent a message
and I'm equal parts excited and scared to get an
answer

10:45
And there it is;
the let down;
the disappointment.
I knew it was coming
deep in my gut
but I still held out hope.
I keep setting myself up
just to keep getting cut down

The drunk man makes promises
the sober man can't keep

11:30
Stomach aches,
anxiety and stress
I'm struggling to find the good in all of this

1:30pm
It keeps coming
I feel sick
I feel disappointment
I feel sadness

3:50
not long now
and I'm going home
to curl up in a ball
and to sleep the rest of the day away.
I can't stand this
moody, needy person
that I feel like I am now...

Jan. '21

Never Ending Sleep (emotional exhaustion)

I'm so tired, but not in a sleepy way
The sort of tired
where I just want to
lay my head on your chest
and not get up…

If They Stay (value)

When I would date a guy and he would love me
"too much"
... I would walk away...

I would cut off contact, I would put my foot
down and refuse to go on anymore, coz I didn't
want my heart broken.

Others I would push them away
I'd find their buttons, their triggers,
anything for them, to get to the point of walking
away

Coz in my mind, I was only worth it,
crazy, or not,
clingy, over the top,
depressed, anxious,
overly loving or not,

I was only worth it
... if they stayed.

Disguise (hiding- again)

I'm smiling
so that they don't see
everything that's broken
deep inside of me

Can't see the pain
that I hide in my eyes
Don't want to hurt them
so I wear a disguise

But if you look close enough
you will surely see,
in the depths of my eyes
that I just want to be free.

Feb 21

Opening Connections (truth)

If I tell you about my past
It's so that you can understand why I am the person that I am
not for you to judge me, or feel sorry for me.

I do it for connection, understanding, honesty and truth
and hopefully from my past, you can see things from a different perspective than your own

Stay

The colourful bruises are long gone,
and the visible scars are unseen by another
But my mind and my heart,
were taking a lot longer to recover.

Lost in our own darkness,
we each bleed out alone.
Too scared to open up to the other,
keeping up walls of stone.

You told me to close my eyes and breathe,
to think what I want to do,
I took a moment to collect my thoughts,
and I realised, I just want you.

I want to climb the mountain with you,
The effort worth it for the reward.
Even if we don't make it to the top
and we can't go any further forward.

Its not going to be easy,
If we choose to take this road.
There'll be ups and downs along the path,
but there's two of us to take the load.

We seemed to choose the hardest time,
to realise what we were.
Emotions running in heightened states,
but I know what I'd prefer.

I know I can't take away your memories
and I can't take away your pain.
Things that haunt us in the night,
might very well remain.

But I'd rather walk beside you,
Even a thousand k's away.
Even when your demons come,
I just want you to stay.

16/4/21

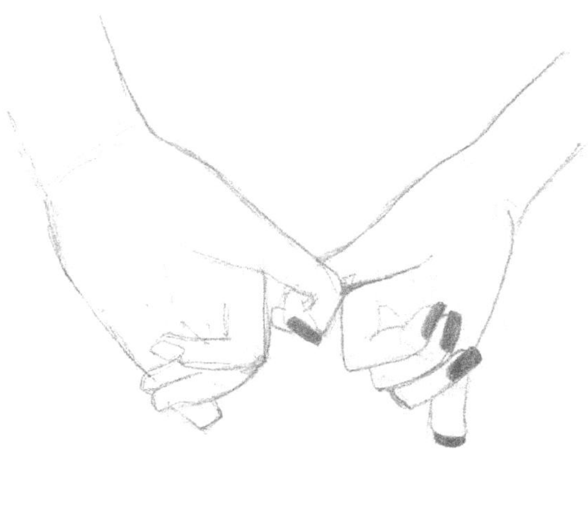

Daylight (opening my eyes)

The shadows came to me
almost every single night
I'd call and I'd cry
as they'd revel in my fright

But in amongst the darkness
I found a little light
someone to tell my secrets to
someone to hold me through the night

Your demons have a hold of you,
won't let you go without a fight
and I tried to be there for you,
I wanted to be your light.

Time it passed by quickly
you became a constant in my world
Then suddenly our demons took over
and around us each they curled

But now my tears fall freely
as I wake to another day
Wishing things were different
and that you hadn't walked away

It would have been easier
If you hadn't opened my eyes
I didn't need to know I loved you
and I could have kept living with lies

Coz now it hurts even more
when you're not with me at night
Coz you told me you loved me
and then left me in the daylight.

Shadows (baggage)

I guess it was always going to end up this way
where we would both hurt, and one of us would
walk away.

When the world around us conspired and tried to
get us to sway
One would always walk on and the other would
stay.

Shadows follow both of us, in dreams and in the
day
But we can't always fight the demons and our
ghosts away

Because they like to remind us, that they will
always stay
Even if we both fight so hard and we never
intended to walk away

It hurts, now that I know, even though I love you
this way,
You're going to keep pushing and that you will
never stay.

The fall (depression)

Don't let go
hold tight to my hand
I'm falling down again
Can't see the ground,
but it's coming up fast.

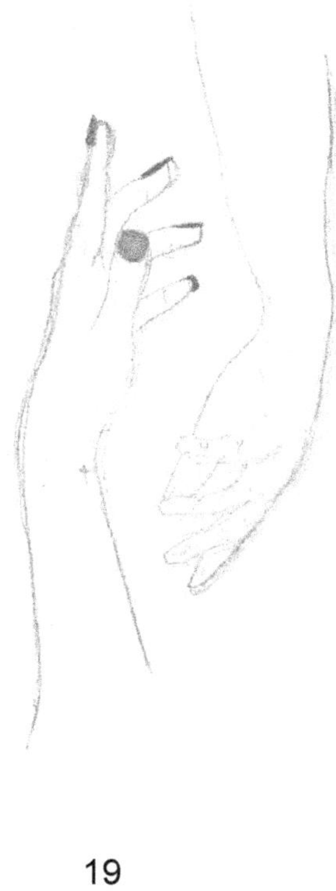

The Split (the inevitable)

I felt it....
The crack,
the split down the middle.
That one moment in time
When I pushed
and you pulled...
right out of my arms.

My Own Lifeline

I don't know you,
and you don't know me.
But you're helping me to open up,
helping me to see.

You're helping me to find,
just a little bit of light.
When my mind is lost and lonely,
you find me in the night.

Your words they make it better,
They become my own lifeline.
Helping me to find myself,
One night at time.

Finding My Roots (home)

Moving away,
I lost all connection.
connection to family
connection to friends
connection to country
connection to self

I focused on what was in front of me,
what I had to do
what I needed to do
for kids
for work
for partner
for everything and everyone, except ME

I lost all peace
and never felt settled
I was always running
to something
from something
for something,
never content to just be.

When I sat
staring up at that windmill,

the breeze in my hair.
I felt it.
Peace.
It settled over me like a blanket
and left me feeling warm
and whole
inside

I breathed in the country air,
my bare toes wriggled in the red-brown dirt
the scuttle of a mouse,
the hens clucking quietly away
and the roosters crow
that interrupts the sunrise

I feel at peace here
The open fields my home
I wrap my arms around myself,
hugging way the cool morning chill.
Staring up at the awakening sky,
I feel a presence at my side.

I'm handed a hot cuppa,
and with thanks my in eyes
I take a sip of the steaming hot liquid.
As we both look out to the view, I hear:
"It's missed you you know"
"I've missed it here too"

As I'm driving down the long dirt driveway
there are tears in my eyes,
but peace in my heart
and the knowledge,
that I'll be coming home again soon.
For this place is my roots
and I'll always come back to my roots.

-Me-

"I miss you,
It's been so long,
I can't really remember you at all"

The Mirror (the silence)

I don't know who I am anymore,
but then I wonder,
Did I ever?
Maybe I didn't,
but always had someone,
or something blocking my emotions and feelings
from coming to the surface.

I was never still enough to feel anything,
never looked close enough in the mirror,
never listened to my inner voice,
She was too quiet,and I was too busy

Now I'm standing here waiting,
waiting for her to talk
and it's like she's lost her voice.
She's silent,
she looks at me in confusion, mixed with a
pleading.

I don't know
I don't know where to start
to find out who I am

Dare You (find your brave)

Dare you to say
whatever's on your mind.
Dare you to tell the truth.
Dare you to say
whatever's in your heart.
But most of all,
I dare you to do what makes you happy

Still Searching for Me

I am not old,
But I feel older than I am.
I have lived more,
and seen more, than I care to admit.
I haven't travelled other countries in the world,
I haven't been on a helicopter or jumped out of a
plane.
I never learned to surf or play the drums
I've forgotten how to ride a bike and play the
piano.

I've been happy and I've been sad
I've been a mess and I've been depressed
But I've gone along, carried myself on
And now I see
It's not about being happy,
or sad,
what I've done, or what I haven't.
It's about being me.

But who is "me"?

Am I a fancy coat?
Or a top hat and cane?
Am I comfy jeans?

Or a ball gown & glass slippers?
Am I active wear?
Or a set of P.J's and fluffy socks?

But why do I have to just pick one?
Why do I have to abide by just one set of rules,
one construct?
Why can't I be spiritual,
without being a specific religion?
Why can't I be Australian.
without being a specific race?
Why can't I be whoever I want to be,
without judgement surrounding me?

The loudest voices are usually the negative,
So maybe I need to turn it down.
Maybe I don't listen to anyone else,
And I search for my inner voice instead.

So who am I?

I have travelled around Australia
Fallen in love (more than once)
Made some mistakes (a lot)
But I have come back from my lows
I can trust now that I am myself;
Because every time my heart gets broken,
or I'm just falling apart,
I keep picking up the pieces

and putting myself back together.

Right now in my life,
I am content
I am on my own, but I am not lonely
I am a mother
I am a daughter, a sister, a granddaughter
I am a niece, an aunty, a sister-in-law,
a loyal friend, a confidant and so much more

But most of all, and more importantly,

I am Emily, I'm 39
And I'm still searching for me.

www.ingramcontent.com/pod-product-compliance
Lightning Source LLC
Chambersburg PA
CBHW051751130826
49812CB00033B/1096
* 9 7 8 9 3 5 7 2 1 1 9 1 8 *